Anatomy of a *Gildy* Episode

The Who's Who of
GG470129 *Marjorie's Hotrod Boyfriend*:
The Great Gildersleeve, John Whedon
and Beyond

Anatomy of a *Gildy* Episode

The Who's Who of
GG470129 *Marjorie's Hotrod Boyfriend*:
The Great Gildersleeve, John Whedon
and Beyond

By Peggy Adler

Anatomy of a Gildy Episode
The Who's Who of GG470129 Marjorie's Hotrod Boyfriend:
The Great Gildersleeve, John Whedon and Beyond

© 2025 Peggy Adler

Published in the United States of America by:
Tiggy Winkle Press

Printer's PDF by PKJ Passion Global

Layout by Peggy Adler

Cover Design by Peggy Adler

ISBN - 979-8-9942406-3-2

Table of Contents

GG470129 *Marjorie's Hotrod Boyfriend*
(https://www.downpour.com/anatomy-of-a-gildy-episode?sp‡141788)

Copy and paste this link into your search engine for a free download of   the original, live January 29, 1947 NBC radio broadcast.

Preface

The Great Gildersleeve was a radio situation comedy spawned from *Fibber McGee and Molly* and was one of the earliest ever spin-offs. The year was 1941.

In *Fibber McGee and Molly*, the character Throckmorton P. Gildersleeve was the bombastic, pompous windbag owner of a girdle factory in Wistful Vista and was introduced to radio audiences in an October 1939 episode. There, he was the antagonist of Fibber McGee and his character became so popular the new series arose featuring the same lead actor in the role of Gildersleeve - Harold Peary.

In the spin-off, which took Gildersleeve from Wistful Vista to Summerfield, Gildersleeve was somewhat mellower and once there, eventually morphed into the town's Water Commissioner with a family – a niece and nephew, whose parents are said to have died in an automobile accident. And thus, there, he headed a household comprised of Marjorie and Leroy Forrester and a housekeeper and cook by the name of Birdie.

The series was initially written by Leonard Levinson, who left the show after the first season. With his departure the team of John Whedon and Sam Moore came on board, eventually becoming the *The Great Gildersleeve's* head writers. Under Whedon and Moore, the show went from having stand-alone episodes to ones that related to others along the way, thereby creating a continuous story line. And Birdie's character slowly developed into the brains and caregiver of the family unit.

John Whedon would eventually go on to write for television for such iconic sit-coms as *The Dick Van Dyke Show, The Donna Reed Show* and *Leave it to Beaver,* among others and garnered two Emmy nominations -- one for *A Night to Remember*, about the sinking of the Titanic, which he wrote with George Roy Hill. And as is common with most, if not all, script writers, Whedon took artistic license and scripted the names of his family, friends and neighbors into one show or another – such as *Marjorie's Hotrod Boyfriend* (*The Great Gildersleeve*), which aired live on January 29, 1947. There, Whedon took advantage of the fact that Gildersleeve's niece's nickname was Marge, the same as his sister's; his sister's husband's name was Richard, the same as that of a new pop song character of the day; and their ten year old son's name -- Jerry Walsh.

GG470129 Marjorie's Hotrod Boyfriend

(The Great Gildersleeve > Aired Live on NBC Radio, January 29, 1947)

Announcer:	The Kraft Foods Company presents *The Great Gildersleeve*.
Gildersleeve:	(belly laugh - followed by a musical interlude)
Announcer:	It's *The Great Gildersleeve*, starring Harold Peary, brought to you by the Kraft Foods Company, makers of Parkay Margarine, and a complete line of famous quality food products.
Announcer:	Now let's get on to Gildersleeve and see what he's up to. It seems to be about 11 o'clock at night, an hour at which, in Summerfield, the citizens have generally heard the last radio program and brushed their teeth, opened their bedroom windows, a discreet crack, and gone to bed. This, in fact, is what Gildersleeve has done, but he'll have trouble going to sleep. He is annoyed.
Gildersleeve:	Darn kid, give her a good talking to in the morning -- gallivanting around at all hours. Hmm. I wonder where she is.
Announcer:	Where is Marjorie? At this moment she is with friends. She is sitting in the front seat of a hopped up jalopy, or hot rod, with a young man named Jerry Walsh, who is driving more or less. In the back seat are a young lady named Francie, and a

young man named Mike something or other. The whole thing sounds something like this. (Very Noisy jalopy sound and kids loudly singing "Open the door Richard. Open the door and let me in. Open the door Richard. Richard, why don't you open the door?")

Jerry Walsh: This is the place, isn't it, Marge?

Marjorie: Yes.

Sound of the jalopy backfiring

Marjorie: Jerry, for heaven's sake, do you want to wake up the whole block?

Francie: Oh whatta we care. Anybody asleep now is a square.

Marjorie: Jerry, please. The house is dark. They're all asleep.

Jerry Walsh: Sorry, Marge, I couldn't stop it.

Marjorie: Well, good night, everybody.

Francie: Good night, Marjorie.

Mike: So long Marge.

Jerry Walsh: I'll go to the door with you.

Jerry walks her to the door and says, "Uh, see you tomorrow night Marge?"

Marjorie:	I don't know. What's going on?
Jerry Walsh:	I don't know. Oh, we'll cook up something.
Marjorie:	What?
Jerry Walsh:	Oh, something. Maybe just the two of us, huh?
Marjorie:	Just the two of us?

From the jalopy come the voices of Mike and Francie

Mike:	Open the door Richard. Let the lady in there.
Francie:	Why don't you open the door?
Marjorie:	They're so smart! Oh my goodness.
Jerry Walsh:	What's the matter?
Marjorie:	I haven't got my key.
Jerry Walsh:	Oh, gosh what do you do about that?
Marjorie:	I'll have to ring and wake him up. You better beat it Jerry. He'll be awful mad when he comes down.
Jerry Walsh:	I'm not afraid of him.

Marjorie:	You're not? Well just the same, it'll be easier if you're not just standing here with me.
Jerry Walsh:	Well OK Marge. Whatever you say. But if he gets tough …
Marjorie:	You'd better go.
Jerry Walsh:	Marge…
Marjorie:	Please go Jerry. I think I hear him coming.
Jerry Walsh:	You do? OK, I'll call you tomorrow. Good night Marge.

Francie – from the jalopy: Open the door Margie. (laughter from the jalopy)

Marjorie:	Oh, go away.

Sound of doorknob turning ..

Gildersleeve:	Well Marjorie ...
Marjorie:	I'm sorry Unky. I thought I had a key.

Sound of the jalopy backfiring and then driving away.

Gildersleeve:	Stop that racket out there. Come in before I freeze to death. (Door closes) Now, I do not propose to discuss your conduct at this time, young lady.

	Decent people like myself have been trying to get some sleep.
Marorie:	I'm sorry, Unky.
Gildersleeve:	As the person who is responsible for your welfare, I need sleep.
Marjorie:	I'm sorry.
Gildersleeve:	Well, you'll be sorrier in the morning. You'll be .... let me smell your breath young lady.
Marjorie:	What for?
Gildersleeve:	Well, lucky thing for you, you haven't been smoking. Now go to bed.

Musical interlude then more jalopy noise and kids laughing

More music ...

The next morning

Leroy:	Hi, Unk.
Gildersleeve:	Good morning Leroy.
Birdie:	Good morning Mr. Gildersleeve. Here's your orange juice and some boiled eggs and three, four pieces of toast. You think they'll carry you?

Gildersleeve:	I guess so. Thank you, Birdie.
Leroy:	Gosh, where's Marge? She'll be late.
Birdie:	I expect she's getting a little extra rest, Leroy.
Gildersleeve:	She didn't get home until the middle of the night. She and some gang of roughnecks hollering and yelling out there in the street after 12 o'clock.
Leroy:	I didn't hear a thing!
Gildersleeve:	You're sub-normal.
Birdie:	Sounds like they were having a lot of fun out there.
Gildersleeve:	Oh, did they wake you up Birdie?
Birdie:	No sir, I was awake, but I heard about that talkin' and laughin'. Sounded like a lot of fun.
Gildersleeve:	That's not the sort of fun we approve Birdie.
Birdie:	No sir. Sound like fun all the same. You know how young folks is Mr. Gildersleeve.
Gildersleeve:	Not necessarily.
Birdie:	Yes sir.
Gildersleeve:	Disgraceful riding around on some kid's motorcycle, backfiring and yelling.

Leroy:	Motorcycle? It was probably a hot rod.
Gildersleeve:	What?
Leroy:	A hot rod. They take a jalopy and hop it up.
Gildersleeve:	Well that makes more noise than anything else (Marjorie enters the kitchen and there's a long pause) Well...
Marjorie:	Good morning, Unky
Leroy:	Hi Marge.
Gildersleeve:	I trust you enjoyed your night's repose Miss Forrester.
Marjorie.	I slept all right.
Gildersleeve:	Oh you did. It might interest you to know that after I went back to bed I didn't sleep a single wink the rest of the night.
Marjorie:	I'm sorry.
Gildersleeve:	Had bad dreams, too.

There's a long pause.

| Marjorie: | Can I have some breakfast? |

Birdie:	Be right in, Miss Marjorie.
Gildersleeve:	Now who was with you last night making all that noise?
Marjorie:	Francie and Jerry and Mike. Mike was Francie's date.
Gildersleeve:	And Jerry was yours. Jerry, who may I ask?
Marjorie:	Jerry Walsh. We were in his car.
Leroy:	I told you Unk. That was Jerry's hopped up Ford.
Gildersleeve:	That will do. Marjorie, I believe I've spoken to you before about that Walsh boy, have I not? I have a definite impression he's fast.
Leroy:	I'll say. He's the fastest guy on the basketball team.
Gildersleeve:	Leroy! I'm talking to your sister. You stay out of this. Marjorie, have I or have I not spoken to you about young Walsh?
Marjorie:	I don't know. You're always speaking to me about somebody.
Gildersleeve:	My dear young lady, you may find it very tiresome, but I'm your guardian. I have a responsibility for your friends.

Marjorie:	There's nothing the matter with Jerry.
Gildersleeve:	I don't know his father.
Marjorie:	Oh, what of it. I suppose I couldn't go around with the Prince of Wales if you didn't know the King.
Gildersleeve:	You're being impertinent. You won't go around with the Prince of Wales either, unless I say so.
Birdie:	Morning Miss Marjorie.
Marjorie:	Good morning, Birdie.
Birdie:	Are you sure you don't want something extra for breakfast honey?
Marjorie:	No, thank you Birdie.
Gildersleeve:	What's this? Orange juice and a half a piece of toast?
Marjorie:	That's all I want.
Gildersleeve:	Well, of all...
Leroy:	She's reducing!
Marjorie:	Leroy. You ....
Gildersleeve:	What's this? What's this? What did you say, Leroy?

Leroy:	Nothing.
Gildersleeve:	Well, by George, young lady, you may think you're big enough to ride around in cars and come in at all hours. But if you've taken up reducing, that's the limit. Reduce what, for heaven's sake? You haven't got anything to reduce.
Marjorie:	Unky, I consider this a personal matter.
Gildersleeve:	Personal my eye. As your guardian I'm also responsible for your health. Bring her some bacon and eggs Birdie.
Birdie:	Yes sir.
Marjorie:	But I don't want them.
Gildersleeve:	Bring her some bacon and eggs. I'd like to remind you, Marjorie, that while you may consider yourself grown up, as a matter of fact, you're still a little girl.
Marjorie:	I'm sixteen.
Gildersleeve:	It'll be five years before you can vote. In the meantime, I want you in bed every night at ten o'clock. Do you understand?
Marjorie:	Unky!
Gildersleeve:	I mean it. Ten o'clock, lights out. No boys hangin' around.

Marjorie:	Unky!
Gildersleeve:	I still mean it.
Leroy:	Oh, for corn's sake.
Gildersleeve:	You stay out of this!
Marjorie:	(Crying) I think you're mean and awful.
Gildersleeve:	(Under his breath) ... confound it, there must be some way to end this.
Marjorie:	(Sobbing) Ahh!
Gildersleeve:	Marjorie.
Marjorie:	(Still Sobbing)
Gildersleeve:	Marjorie. Perhaps I was a little harsh just now. But don't you see I'm trying to look out for your own good? Older people know things that you haven't been able to learn yet. I've learned them in the hard school of experience. I'm just trying to save you from heartaches, that's all.
Marjorie:	(Still sobbing) You don't know anything.
Gildersleeve:	My dear, I'll take back the punishment. By being in at ten o'clock.

Marjorie:	What about the boys?
Gildersleeve:	Well, I'll take that back, too. I'm weak, I guess. But for your own sake, can't you find someone nicer than this Walsh boy? What about Ben Waterford? Now, there's a nice boy. Why don't you see him anymore?
Marjorie:	Ben's all right ... only. I don't know ....he's not very exciting.
Gildersleeve:	Exciting boys are no good, my dear, in the long run. Ben is a fine, manly boy. What's the matter with Ben?
Marjorie:	He never can think of anything to do - except go to the movies.
Gildersleeve:	Well, What's the matter with that?
Marjorie:	... and when you get to the movies ... he... well, he just watches the movie.
Gildersleeve:	My dear.
Marjorie:	I just mean he never talks or anything. He never can think of anything to say.
Gildersleeve:	Well, uh...... the still water runs deep Marjorie!
Marjorie:	Deep! He's just dull. He never.....

Doorbell rings

Leroy:	Doorbell.
Marjorie:	Quarter to nine. That's Francie calling for me.
Gildersleeve:	Leroy, you let her in. Your sister's got to eat something.
Leroy:	Okay.
Marjorie:	Do I look as if I've been ...
Gildersleeve:	No. No one would ever guess it.
Leroy:	Hi, Francie. Come on in. Marge is finishing her breakfast.
Marjorie:	It's late. Just go in.
Francie:	Marge ..... Oh, good morning, Mr. Gildersleeve.
Gildersleeve:	Good morning, Francie. How's your mother?
Francie:	She's fine, thank you.
Gildersleeve:	Father, get over that cold, all right?
Francie:	Oh yes, he went back to the office yesterday. I hope we didn't disturb you last night bringing Marjorie home.

Gildersleeve:	Well, I know how young folks are.
Leroy:	Hah!
Gildersleeve:	Leeeeroy! You may run along to school.
Leroy:	Okay. So long Marge. So long Francie. Hey, Birdie, did I leave my coat in the kitchen?
Gildersleeve:	Have a chair, Francie. As I was saying, I think I understand, young people. But I was just asking Marjorie why she didn't see more of Ben Waterford. I think he's a fine boy, don't you?
Francie:	Oh, sure. Ben's all right. But he's so dull. He never can think of anything to do. The movies.
Marjorie:	That's just what I was telling Unky. There's just nothing exciting about him.
Francie:	Oh, that's funny.
Marjorie:	What's funny?
Francie:	Well, I'm only telling you this because maybe you ought to know. But Ben says the same thing about you.
Marjorie:	What?
Francie:	He says you're all right, but not very exciting.

Marjorie:	Well, of all the nerve. Who did he say this to?
Francie:	Louise. He's been going around with her lately. She told me, and I thought as a friend ....
Marjorie:	Thanks, Francie. Well, I saw them a couple of times in the library, but I never thought... Louise. And he says I'm dull. Well, I'll show Mr. Ben who's dull.
Gildersleeve:	Marjorie ....
Marjorie:	I suppose he thinks I'm just a quiet little mouse or something. Well, he'll find out.
Francie:	Oh, Marjorie, I think all he said was that you were conventional.
Marjorie:	Conventional? That's the worst of all. I'll show him. I'll go out with Jerry Walsh tonight. Where's my coat?
Gildersleeve:	Marjorie ... breakfast.
Marjorie:	I've eaten all I can stand. I'll go out with Jerry tonight. And don't worry, Unky, I'll have a key this time. If I come home at all.
Gildersleeve:	Marjorie! Now, what am I going to do?
Musical Interlude	
Announcer:	We'll get back to *The Great Gildersleeve* and his problem in just a minute.

	Isn't it amazing how a little extra something added to your favorite recipe can give it a lot more appetite appeal?
Female Voice:	That's certainly true, Mr. Laing. We women are always looking for simple, new ways to improve our meals.
Announcer:	Well, if that's the case, I'll bet you'd like something I saw tried in the Kraft kitchen recently. It's a simple recipe to make biscuits better with just two easy tricks.
Female Voice:	Did you say, two easy tricks?
Announcer:	Yes, and they're both very simple. The first trick is to add Kraft grated cheese to your regular biscuit mix. That's an extra something that lifts them out of the ordinary. The second trick is even simpler. It's to serve these luscious cheese biscuits with delicious, flavor-fresh Parkay margarine to make them taste extra good. Parkay's fresh country sweet flavor is preferred by millions for biscuits, bread, pancakes, and waffles. So for all those favorite breads you bake or buy, insist on the margarine of Kraft quality. Look first when you shop for delicious, nourishing Parkay. P-A-R-K-A-Y. Parkay margarine made by Kraft.

Musical Interlude

Announcer:	Now let's return to *The Great Gildersleeve*. We'll have to follow him to Peavey's pharmacy.

Peavey:	A little lemon, a teaspoon of soda, half a glass of hot water every morning without fail. That's how I avoid colds. (Peavey coughs twice)
Gildersleeve:	Yes. Yes. Peavey, tell me something. Does a boy named Jerry Walsh ever come in here?
Peavey:	Well, yes. Quite frequently ...
Gildersleeve:	I thought so.
Peavey:	.... But then, so do most of the boys. Why?
Gildersleeve:	I haven't got any use for him.
Peavey:	That so? Why?
Gildersleeve:	I haven't got any use for the kind of boy who hangs around drugstores.
Peavey:	Well, I wouldn't say that. Your own nephew has been known to come in here.
Gildersleeve:	That's different.
Peavey:	In fact he seems to do a good part of his reading here. Right on the floor, there, in front of my magazine rack.
Gildersleeve:	I'll speak to him about that. Right now I'm talking about this Walsh boy.

Peavey:	Why are you suddenly interested in Jerry Walsh?
Gildersleeve:	I'm not. It's my niece.
Peavey:	Oh.
Gildersleeve:	What kind of a boy is he Peavey?
Peavey:	Sounds to me as if you've already made up your mind.
Gildersleeve:	Not at all. I'm perfectly willing to be open minded. I just don't like the fellow that's all.
Peavey:	Oh. Oh.
Gildersleeve:	But you say he comes in here all the time. You must have some idea. What's he like?
Peavey:	Well, it's hard to say. I'd say he's a good deal like other boys.
Gildersleeve:	Well, that's no help.
Peavey:	Well, they come in here .... they sit around ... three or four of them ..... usually drink Cokes.
Gildersleeve:	I thought so!
Peavey:	I will say, he seems a little free with his money.
Gildersleeve:	Oh, a waster. I thought as much.

Peavey: Oh, I wouldn't say that. It seems to be more a spirit of generosity. He's the one who usually offers to pay for the drinks. And the others usually let him.

Gildersleeve: I know the type. A good time, Charlie. Those fellows don't fool me. What else do you know about him?

Peavey: I hear he had a little bad luck yesterday. I hear he had his driver's license taken away from him.

Gildersleeve: Well, it's about time. By, George, I'm glad to hear that. The way these kids go tearing around in these ..... collapsies, or whatever they call them. There oughta be a law.

Peavey: I can go with you there.

Gildersleeve: Had his license taken away, huh? Serves him right. Now, why can't Marjorie just stick to a nice boy like Ben Waterford? You don't catch Ben whooping around town, hollering and backfiring at all hours of the night.

Peavey: Well, I don't believe Ben even owns a car, does he?

Gildersleeve: That's one of the nicest things about it. But this Jerry, by George I'm glad they clipped his wings. Serves him good and right.

Footsteps

Floyd enters the pharmacy

Floyd:	Serves who good and right?
Peavey:	Well, if it isn't Floyd Munson.
Gildersleeve:	Hello, Floyd.
Floyd:	Hi, Commissioner. Give us a pack of Fatima's, Peave. That's a good kid. Well Commissioner....
Gildersleeve:	Well Floyd ...
Floyd:	You're getting a little shaggy around the ears there. I ought to be seeing you in a couple of days.
Gildersleeve:	I have more on my mind than just my hair Floyd.
Floyd:	Hah! Yeah it's pretty good. He must have been listening to the radio Peave.
Peavey.	He don't just think up them smart cracks by himself
Cash register ringing	
Gildersleeve:	Floyd, do you know a boy named Jerry Walsh?
Floyd:	Jerry Walsh? Yeah. He plays center on the basketball team. Parts his hair in the middle. Sure I know him.
Gildersleeve:	What do you think of him?

Floyd:	Good kid.
Gildersleeve:	You would.
Floyd:	What's the matter with him?
Peavey:	He's having a little family difficulty.
Floyd:	He thinks he's got difficulty.
Gildersleeve:	Don't ever have a niece, Floyd.
Floyd:	Don't ever have a wife -- huh, Peave?
Peavey:	Now, I wouldn't say that Floyd.
Floyd:	What's the matter, Commissioner? The niece getting ideas?
Gildersleeve:	She was born with ideas. She won't listen to anybody else's. I can't do a thing with her.
Floyd:	Commissioner, that's the story of my life -- me and Lovey.
Peavey:	That's the story of mankind.
Floyd:	What's that Peave?
Peavey:	Nothing.

Floyd:	Yep, It's like I say. They're all the same. Wife, niece, sweetheart, mother-in-law. They'll really lead you on a chase if you let them.
Gildersleeve:	How do you stop them?
Floyd:	You gotta know how.
Gildersleeve:	Well, how?
Floyd:	Pay no attention to them. That burns them up worse than anything ....
Gildersleeve:	That's not what I'm after, exactly.
Floyd:	... Like with me and Lovey. I come home at night and right away I see she's in one of her mean streaks. I ain't hardly in the door and she sticks her jaw out and says, "I think I'll have mom over for the weekend".
Gildersleeve:	Well...
Floyd:	Now in the old days, I would have given her an argument. But not anymore. I got smart.
Gildersleeve:	Well, what do you do?
Floyd:	Commissioner she don't want the old ... She don't want her mom over any more than I do. She just wants to start a fight. Well I don't give her the satisfaction. She gets no arguments from me.

	When Lovey starts up with me like that, all I do is yes her to death.
Gildersleeve:	(bellylaugh)
Floyd:	Go ahead, I says. Invite her over. Glad to see her. Have your Pop over, too. Send for the whole family. Tell them to stay a couple of months. Glad to have „em.
Peavey:	Floyd, you're an old rascal.
Floyd:	Well, I'm not so dumb.
Gildersleeve:	And it works?
Floyd:	Like a charm! You can write it down in your book Commissioner. When a dame is in one of them moods, anything you say, she's going to do the opposite. That right Peavey?
Peavey:	Floyd -- yes, that seems to be.
Gildersleeve:	You know, you fellas have given me a new slant! Yes sir, by George. Yes sir. (belly laugh)

Musical interlude

Gildersleeve enters his house (door closing)

Gildersleeve:	Well, this is a pretty little picture, I must say.
Leroy:	Hi Unk.

Gildersleeve:	Leroy at his school books. Marjorie at hers. Nobody fighting. Quite a treat. How does it happen, my dear, that you're not off with your friend Jerry? Cat got our tongue? Too bad. Leroy, perhaps you can take time off from your studies to answer your old uncle.
Leroy:	Yeah, what do you want to know?
Gildersleeve:	Nothing in particular. I'll just hang up my things here first. (Closet door closes) Well, Leroy, quite a feat having our sister at home here with us in the evening, isn't it? We've seen so little of her lately.
Leroy:	Are you kidding?
Gildersleeve:	I suppose it's too much to hope that she'll honor us by staying to supper. Lost in her studies. You must be careful not to disturb her, Leroy. By the way, I heard a very sad piece of news this afternoon, Leroy. Very sad. Concerns Jerry Walsh. You recall Jerry Walsh -- a friend of your sister's, I believe?
Leroy:	What's going on here anyway?
Gildersleeve:	It seems, Leroy, that young Master Walsh has had

his driver's license taken away from him. Very sad. Won't be able to drive anymore.

Marjorie: All right, you think you're very smart Uncle Mort. But it might just interest you to know this. I'm sticking by Jerry. I'm sticking by him through thick and thin. And the more trouble he gets into, the more I'll stick by him.

Gildersleeve: I think that's very commendable.

Marjorie: What?

Gildersleeve: I like to see loyalty in a girl. I think you should stick by him.

Marjorie: Well, I will.

Gildersleeve: Well, you should.

Marjorie: All right. I will.

Leroy: What's going on here?

Gildersleeve: After all, the poor boy has been unfairly deprived of his license. He needs sympathy. Maybe he did knock over a few fire hydrants. Is that any reason to take his license away from him?

Marjorie: Uncle Mort, you may think you're joking, but I'm not. I like Jerry Walsh. I like him very much.

Gildersleeve: Good. Then I think you should marry him.

Marjorie:	What? Uncle Mort, really!
Gildersleeve:	I mean it. Marry him right now why don't you. Now. Tonight. Or tomorrow at the latest.
Marjorie:	For two cents, I would.
Gildersleeve:	Elope, why don't you. I'll help you. I'll make all the arrangements. Leroy will help too.
Leroy:	Yeah, I'll hold the ladder.
Marjorie:	You both think you're very funny, don't you?
Birdie:	Mr. Gildersleeve, it's all ready. You want to carve the roast at the table? Or do you want me to hack it up out in the kitchen?
Gildersleeve:	Birdie, please.
Birdie:	Yes sir!
Gildersleeve:	This is a very solemn moment, Birdie. Let's not talk of food.
Marjorie:	Oh, don't listen to him, Birdie.
Gildersleeve:	She's nervous, that's all. And only natural. You see, our little bird is about to fly the coop.
Birdie:	Huh?

Leroy:	Marge's getting married. Aren't you, Marge?
Birdie:	What?
Gildersleeve:	Birdie ... shhh. It's very secret. They're eloping. I'm not even supposed to know. Only I'm helping them. (belly laugh)
Birdie:	Is everybody crazy around here?
Marjorie:	Yes.
Gildersleeve:	Now what I want you to do, Birdie – I want you to run up to Marjorie's room and pack a bag for her. Everything she'll need to elope with.
Marjorie:	That will not be necessary. I'll pack it myself.
Leroy:	Hey, wait!
Gildersleeve:	Let her go.
Leroy:	Hey, you're not gonna let her do it, Unk?
Gildersleeve:	Don't you worry. Your old uncle knows what he's doing.
Birdie:	I wonder.

Musical Interlude

Gildersleeve:	I guess you can clear the table if you want to, Birdie. It appears that Marjorie will not be down.

Birdie:	Mr. Gildersleeve, if you don't mind me saying so. Seems like you're kind of putting your foot in it, if you don't mind me saying so.
Gildersleeve:	Why do you say that?
Birdie:	That ain't no way to treat a girl, the way you're doing it.
Gildersleeve:	Birdie, when a girl gets notions in her head, there's only one thing to do. Kid her out of it.
Birdie:	You could kid her into it.
Gildersleeve:	That shows how much you know. As long as I keep urging her Birdie, she'll never in the world go through with it. I guarantee it. That's the way girls work.
Birdie:	It is?
Gildersleeve:	Anybody knows that.
Birdie:	Mr. Gildersleeve, let me ask you one question.
Gildersleeve:	Mm-hmm?
Birdie:	Was you ever a girl?
Gildersleeve:	Now, Birdie, you just leave everything to me.
Leroy:	Quiet, here comes Marge.

Gildersleeve:	Well, my dear. All ready, I see. I suppose Jerry will be along any minute. Have you called him? I think you ought to call him, don't you?
Marjorie:	I'll call him when I get good and ready.
Birdie:	Oh, Mr. Gildersleeve!
Gildersleeve:	I'll call her bluff Birdie. It's the only way.
Birdie:	Oh, Miss Marjorie, couldn't you eat just a little somethin'?
Gildersleeve:	Yes. Better have a bite before you go, my dear. You're a long time married, you know.
Marjorie:	I'm not hungry, thank you.
Gildersleeve:	Well, she's just excited. You can't blame her. Girl just about to be married. (he laughs) Your overcoat's on the hall table. Don't forget it when you go.
Marjorie:	Thanks a lot!

Sound of a noisy, backfiring jalopy

Leroy:	Hey, what's that?
Gildersleeve:	What?

Jalopy backfires again

Leroy:	That noise! It's Jerry's car.
Gildersleeve:	What the ...
Birdie:	I told you.
Gildersleeve:	I don't care. She'll never go through with it. Well there he is my dear. His car's outside. You mustn't keep him waiting. No time to say goodbye, I guess. Better just run along. Write to us if you get a chance. Well aren't you going?
Marjorie:	All right, I will!
Gildersleeve:	Marjorie! Marjorie, come back here. Marjorie, I didn't mean it, Marjorie. Please, please, come back.
Marjorie:	Let go of me.
Gildersleeve:	Don't go, my dear, please. Oh, Marjorie.
Marjorie:	Oh, Unky (crying)
Gildersleeve:	My dear, you wouldn't leave your old uncle.
Marjorie:	I thought you were going to make me.
Gildersleeve:	I'm nothing but a big fat fool. Don't ever leave us, will you?
Marjorie:	Never! Never!
Gildersleeve:	Don't ever listen to a single word I say.

Marjorie crying

Gildersleeve: Oh, here comes Jerry. Better blow your nose.

Marjorie: You got a handkerchief?

Gildersleeve: Here.

Footsteps

Ben: Hi Marge!

Marjorie: Ben?

Ben: Hi, Mr. Gildersleeve.

Marjorie: It isn't Jerry! It's Ben.

Ben: Hi.

Gildersleeve: Ben. Ben, my boy. How are you? Glad to see you. By George, you're a sight for sore eyes. How are you anyway?

Ben: I'm all right.

Marjorie: Ben, where'd you get the car? I thought it was ... I mean .... it's just that... where'd you get it?

Ben: I borrowed it from a fella. He wasn't going to be using for a few months, so we made a deal. Would you like take a ride?

Marjorie:	Oh, would I!
Ben:	All right, where would you like to go?
Marjorie:	I don't know. Where would you like to go?
Ben:	I don't care. Where would you like to go?
Marjorie:	Makes no difference to me. Where would you like to go?
Ben:	Wherever you'd like to go.
Marjorie:	Well...
Ben:	Would you wanna to go to the movies?
Marjorie:	Oh, Ben, I'd just love to!
Gildersleeve:	The movies ..... (belly laugh)
Ben:	That is, if it's all right with you, Mr. Gildersleeve.
Gildersleeve:	Oh, take her, my boy, and God bless you.
Ben:	Oh, thanks. Shall we go, Marge?
Marjorie:	Good night Unky.
Gildersleeve:	Good night, my dear. Have you forgiven your old uncle?
Marjorie:	Forgiven you? It was all my fault.

Gildersleeve:	No it wasn't, It was mine.
Marjorie:	No, it wasn't. It was mine.
Gildersleeve:	All right. It was yours.
Marjorie:	No, it wasn't. It was yours.
Gildersleeve:	(Giggle) Run along.
Marjorie:	Let's hurry, Ben. We might make the first show. What's playing? Do you know?
Ben:	Something called "Boys' Ranch".
Gildersleeve:	Ah, little Marjorie, going to the movies with her fella.

Car backfires and then drives away

Gildersleeve:	Well, at least it isn't that Jerry.

Musical Interlude

Announcer:	We'll hear from *The Great Gildersleeve* again very shortly. Your menu for breakfast may change from day to day because all of us like variety in foods. But whether you have toast, sweet rolls, pancakes or waffles, I'm sure you'll agree it's the spread that makes them taste extra good. And that's why so many homemakers look first for Parkay margarine. It's so fresh and country sweet in flavor. So delicious in all those favorite hot breads you serve for breakfast or any other meal of the day. Parkay margarine is wonderfully nourishing too.

High in food energy and fortified with 15,000 units of important vitamin A in every single pound. So for a quality spread for bread that's high in good nourishment, rich in good flavor, look first for Parkay. P-A-R-K-A-Y. Parkay margarine made by the Kraft Foods Company.

Musical Interlude

Judge Horace Hooker comes into the Gildersleeve' house

Gildersleeve: Well, good morning, Judge. Come in. Sit down. Have a prune. Ah - Birdie, go coddle an egg for the Judge.

Judge Hooker: No, no, nothing for me, thank you. I've already breakfasted.

Gildersleeve: Well, sit down anyway. You can watch me eat. What's on your mind Horace? You look like the devil.

Judge Hooker: Bad night last night. Bad night.

Gildersleeve: I slept like a baby myself

Judge Hooker: Well, I might have, if some young maniac hadn't come tearing down my street in the middle of the night with his cut-out wide open. Enough to wake the dead.

Gildersleeve: (belly laugh)

Judge Hooker: You won't think it's so funny, perhaps, when I tell you that he had a girl in the car with him and the girl was none other than your niece, Marjorie. Well, aren't you going to say something? Are you going to let your niece tear around at all hours of the night raising heck and disturbing the peace?

Gildersleeve: Judge, I pray to heaven that I may never be so old, so dried up, so forgetful of my own youth, that I would want to rob children of their fun.

Judge Hooker: Well!

Gildersleeve: Good morning, Judge. Good night, folks.

Announcer: *The Great Gildersleeve* is played by Harold Peary. It is written by John Whedon and Sam Moore. The music is by Jack Meakin. Included in the cast are: Walter Tetley as Leroy; Louise Erickson as Marjorie: and Lillian Randolph as Bertie. Earle Ross is Judge Hooker, and Dick LeGrand plays Mr. Peavey. Stay tuned in now for *Duffy's Tavern*. This is John Laing saying good night for the Kraft Foods Company and inviting you to listen in again next Wednesday for the further adventures of *The Great Gildersleeve*.

Music, then:
Chocolate, strawberry, pineapple, even coffee, ice cream. Make any kind you like right in your own refrigerator or home freezer. It's easy with Frizz. Frizz, F-R-I-Z-Z, is a new Kraft product that gives you delicious, satiny smooth ice cream, rich with plenty of milk and cream. For vanilla, all you do is add water, a little sugar, and freeze according to directions on the package. Flavor variations are simple. Frizz is made by an exclusive process that

retains the fresh cream flavor. Be sure to ask for Frizz. Six generous servings from one small package.

This is NBC, the National Broadcasting Company.
(NBC's three chimes)

[Transcription by Peggy Adler, January 2025]

John Ogden Whedon as an infant

John Ogden Whedon

Whedon is a surname that came to England during the 11th century wave of migration, set off by the Norman Conquest of 1066. The name itself is believed to come from the Old English words "hwaee" (wheat) and "denu" (valley) or "dūn" (hill).

*****   *****   *****

John Ogden Whedon's family arrived in British colonial America on February 24, 1644 in the person of a youthful apprentice by the name of Thomas Wheadon, who was born near Axminster, Devon, England in 1636. He debarked at New Haven, which that year had become a colony contiguous with the Connecticut Colony. Early records indicate that young Wheadon apprenticed himself to John Meigs, who promised to teach the lad the trade of tanning over a period of seven years. Yet after their arrival in the colonies, Meigs transferred his contract with young Wheadon to a man by the name of Matthew Gilbert, who failed to teach the lad a trade of any kind. Thus, in 1658, Thomas Wheadon filed a law suit claiming he'd been promised a trade and that other servant's contracts were for four years – while his was for seven. The court ruled that since he was a minor when under indenture, he did not have the authority to contract himself to Meigs in the first place, therefore determining that the contract with Gilbert had been properly fulfilled. In 1661, Thomas married and he and his family were among the first settlers of Branford (originally called Totokett), when a new Plantation Covenant was signed in 1667, of which Thomas Wheadon was a signatory. And by now, he finally was a tanner by trade.

Almost two centuries after Thomas Wheadon arrived in the colonies, his direct descendants eliminated the "a", thereby changing their surname from Wheadon to Whedon. One of the earliest, who came into this world with the new surname, was Maria Whedon, born in 1809. Another, her brother, Nathan Wilson Whedon, born in 1813. By now, this branch of the family lived in Oberlin, Ohio.

Maria Whedon married a doctor by the name of Alexander Steele and one of their sons, John Whedon Steele, went on to win the Congressional Medal of Honor for his service as a volunteer in the Union Army during the Civil War. Colonel Steele married in 1867 and one of his daughters, Marion Jameson Steele, born in 1875, was John Ogden Whedon's mother.

Maria's brother Nathan married as well, and had a son by the name of Charles Ogden Whedon. He, in turn, married in 1875 and his second child, born in 1878, was a son by the name of Burt Denison Whedon. The family lived in Nebraska and Burt matriculated at the State University at Lincoln, but left in his junior year to enlist in the National Guard – serving in the Far East during the Philippine-American War. After returning home, he entered Harvard Law School and upon graduation, being attracted by the glamor of the big city, went to New York to practice. He and his cousin Marion Jameson Steele were married the following year and their son John arrived on the scene eleven months later.

John Ogden Whedon was born November 5, 1905, in New York City's Borough of Manhattan, the oldest of Burt Denison Whedon and Marion Jameson (Steele) Whedon's four children. Eventually, the family moved to suburbia, in the New York City Borough of Queens, to an exclusive community known as Jamaica Estates, where John spent his childhood. Additionally, the family vacationed at a farm they owned in Litchfield, Connecticut.

In the fall of 1923, John matriculated at Harvard, the same university from which his father Burt had received his law degree two decades earlier. At Harvard, John was on the literary board of the school's undergraduate magazine, the *Harvard Lampoon* and by 1926 was its president. While at Harvard, he was also a member of the university's Hasty Pudding Club, which staged musicals written, composed and produced by the students. Upon graduation in 1927, John returned to New York City, where he began to work as a writer and editor for several magazines, including the *New Yorker*, for which he later served as managing editor in the early 1930s.

In June 1931 John married Louise Carroll Angell and the following year their son, Thomas Avery Whedon was born. Six months before John and Carroll married, his brother Roger committed suicide. He was all of 23. Roger, too, had matriculated at Harvard and served on the *Lampoon*'s literary board, graduating two years after John, in 1929.

By 1935, John, Caroll and Tom were living with John's parents in his childhood home on Croydon Road, in Jamaica Estates. Later that year, *Life's Too Short*, a comedy by John Whedon and Arthur Caplan, opened on Broadway – and closed after only ten performances. It would be more than a decade before John ventured back to Broadway. The following year, John and Carroll's daughter Julia (aka Jill) arrived and toward the end of the 1930s, John began to write for radio.

1940 rolled around and the census taken that year had John, Carroll, Tom and Jill still living at the Croydon Road address. August 31, 1941, *The Great Gildersleeve* began to air on NBC radio. Initially, the show was written by Leonard Levinson, but he resigned one year later to work for the United States Office of War Information. Thus, in August 1942, John and new writing partner, Sam Moore, came on board, eventually becoming *The Great Gildersleeve's* head writers.

John's next Broadway foray was a musical titled *Texas Li'l Darlin'*, which opened on November 25, 1949 at the Mark Hellinger Theater. He and his *Gildy* writing partner Sam Moore wrote the book. The music was by Robert Emmett Dolan and the lyrics by Johnny Mercer. The show ran for almost a year, closing on September 9, 1950 after 293 performances.

By now, John had begun the transition from radio to television, as this new medium was beginning to become popular in American households. His first televised credit was for CBS' *54th Street Revue* (aka *Fifty-Fourth Street Revue*), which aired live from a theater on 54th Street in New York City.

According to the census of April 1, 1950, John, Carroll and their kids were living at Pelham, NY, the Westchester County town where Carroll had grown up. Though by August 1954, they were divorced and John had relocated to California in order to continue to write for television. From 1949 forward, he is known to have written and/or adapted the following:

1949, *The Fifty-Fourth Street Review* (one episode)

1949, *Tonight on Broadway* (one episode: Book, *Texas Li'l Darlin'*)

1950, *Musical Comedy Time* (one episode)

1951-1955, *Lux Video Theatre* (eight episodes)

1953, *Hollywood Opening Night* (one episode)

1953, *The Plymouth Playhouse* (one episode)

1954, *My Favorite Husband* (two episodes)

1957, *The Alcoa Hour*

1956-1957, Writer, *Kraft Theatre* (five episodes)
1957, Primetime Emmy nomination, Best Teleplay Writing:
A Night to Remember - One Hour or More, shared with
George Roy Hill.

1958-1960, *The United States Steel Hour* (two episodes)

1958-1962, *The Donna Reed Show* (thirty-nine episodes)

1958-1959, *Leave it to Beaver* (two episodes)

1960-1961, *Sunday Showcase* (two episodes)

1960-1961, *Our American Heritage* (two episodes)

1962, *Dr. Kildare* (one episode)

1962-1963, *Fair Exchange* (four episodes)

1962-1966, *The Dick Van Dyke Show* (seven episodes)
1965 Nominee, Writers Guild of America Award/WGA Award
(TV): Episodic Comedy, *Turtles, Ties and Toreadors* (1963)

1963-1964, *The Andy Griffith Show* (eight episodes)

1965, *Karen* (one episode)

1965-1976, *The Magical World of Disney* (six episodes)

1969, *Room 222* (one episode)

1969, *That Girl*, writer (one episode)

1972, Teleplay, *Young Doctor Kildare* (one episode)

1974, Screenplay, *Island at the Top of the World*

1974, Screenplay, *The Bears and I*

On November 21, 1991, John Ogden Whedon died at the age of 86. He was survived by his son **Thomas Avery Whedon**, his daughter Julia Whedon and his grandchildren, Matthew Thomas Whedon, Samuel Whedon, **Joseph Hill Whedon (aka Joss)**, Jed Tucker Whedon, Zachary Whedon, Erika Schickel and Jessica Schickel.

Glossary

A Night to Remember was an American television play written by **John Whedon** and **George Roy Hill**, which aired live, on NBC's *Kraft Television Theatre*, on March 28, 1956. The teleplay was based upon the book of the same name, written by Walter Lord, depicting the last night on the Titanic and was directed by **George Roy Hill**. The production was nominated for five Prime Time Emmy Awards, including best writing – and won the Emmy for live camera work. Additionally, the show won two Sylvania Television Awards as the year's best television adaptation, as well as for best technical production. The live airing had 107 actors and made use of 31 studio sets – making it the most intricate television production ever attempted, at that point in time.

British colonial America was the period from 1585 to 1783 when the English established colonies in what today is The United States of America. The British sent colonists, convicts, religious dissenters and adventurers to the colonies.

Captain Kangaroo was an American children's television program created by Bob Keeshan in 1955, that ran for twenty-nine seasons on CBS. Keeshan also played the title role. Previously, he created the character of Clarabell the Clown for NBC's *The Howdy Doody Show*. **Tom Whedon** and **Jon Stone** met while working as writers for *Captain Kangaroo* and continued their professional association for decades after leaving the show. *Captain Kangaroo* was the longest running children's TV show, until it was surpassed by *Mister Rogers Neighborhood* – which itself, was later surpassed by *Sesame Street*. Though at this writing, *Captain Kangaroo* still holds the record for episode count, with 6,090.

Fifty-Fourth Street Revue was an American variety television program that was broadcast on CBS from May 5, 1949, through March 25, 1950. The program was a "showcase for up-and-coming professionals", originating from a theater on 54th Street in New York City.

George Roy Hill wrote the Emmy nominated script for Kraft Theatre's production of *A Night to Remember,* with **John Ogden Whedon**, and also directed the dramatization, which aired live on NBC. The production brought Hill to the attention of a Broadway producer, who brought him on board to direct *Look Homeward Angel* – which garnered him a Tony nomination. This success led to his featured film directorial debut with *Period of Adjustment.*

George Roy Hill was born and raised in Minneapolis, Minnesota and after prep school went on to college in New Haven, Connecticut, where among other things, he was in the Yale Glee Club and president of the Yale Dramat. He also sang with Yale's Whiffenpoofs and Spizzwinks – and belonged to a Secret Society there known as Scroll and Key. After college he served in World War II, was recalled for service during the Korean War and under the G.I. Bill, matriculated at a graduate school in Ireland. Upon his return to the States, he studied theater in New York, where he acted in plays both on and off Broadway. And it was Hill's acting that first brought him to Kraft Theatre. George Roy Hill went on to an extraordinary motion picture directorial career, with credits including *The World of Henry Orient*, *Thoroughly Modern Millie, Butch Cassidy and the Sundance Kid*, *The Sting, The Great Waldo Pepper, Slapshot, A Little Romance* and *The World According To Garp.*

Hollywood Opening Night was an American anthology television program that was broadcast on CBS in 1951-1952 and on NBC in 1952-1953. The NBC version was the first dramatic anthology presented live from the West Coast. Episodes were 30 minutes long.

The Lux Video Theatre originated in 1950 as a half hour show and was a spin-off from the popular *Lux Radio Theater* series, which had broadcast from 1934 to 1955. In September 1953 *Lux Video Theatre* relocated from New York to California, where they aired on NBC for the next four years. With the introduction of a one-hour format and the move to Hollywood, abridged versions of popular films were often used as the basis for shows.

Money - a Musical Play for Cabaret was written by **Tom Whedon** and David Axelrod, with music by Sam Pottle and its original copyright date was 1963, as an unpublished work. Tom later worked with Axelrod on *The Dick Cavett Show. Money* was first presented at New York City's Upstairs at the Downstairs on July 9, 1963. In the cast was **Jon Stone**.

Money is comprised of skits that could easily have been staged as individual numbers in a revue. One is a takeoff on doctors as businessmen. Another is a satire on organizations and associations, ranging from the right wing "John Birchers to left-wing kooks". Yet another is a take-off on philanthropic organizations and charities. As for the storyline – it's about a wealthy young man who is spurred on by the woman he loves to make something of himself. Pushed on by her, he finds that the working world, the professional world and the institutional world are often dominated by grasping, greedy men and women. Though he fails at everything he attempts to do, it all works out in the end as she will accept him as a complete failure.

Sam Moore was **John Ogden Whedon's** *Great Gildersleeve'* writing partner. They also teamed up as co-authors of the book for Broadway's *Texas Li'l Darlin'*. Moore was the founder and president of the Radio Writers Guild and was blacklisted after refusing to answer questions before the House Committee on Un-American Activities. He died of a heart attack in October 1989 at the age of eighty-five.

Open The Door Richard*,* the song being sung by the kids in Marjorie's boyfriend's hotrod, was recorded and released in October 1946. The earliest known version to hit *Billboard's* Best Seller Chart did so on January 31, 1947, two days after the song had aired live in *Marjorie's Hotrod Boyfriend* in the hit radio series, *The Great Gildersleeve.* The song stayed there for five weeks, peaking at number three. By February 7, 1947 another recorded version found itself on *Billboard's* Best Seller Chart as well, lasting there for four weeks, eventually peaking at number one. And two other versions were there one week later, one lasting on the chart for two weeks, peaking at number seven and the other there for three weeks, topping out at number four. Did this song's inclusion in the *Gildersleeve* script assist its meteoric rise to the top of the charts? Regardless, the song began as a black vaudeville routine, performed by black comedians, in blackface, no less – and was made famous in a short film -- as well as on the stage, at theaters like the Apollo, in New York City's Harlem.

Colonel John Whedon Steele served as a volunteer in the Union Army during the Civil War and was awarded the Congressional Medal of Honor for his actions of November 29, 1864 as a Major and Aide-de-Camp, at Spring Hill, Tennessee. There, during a night attack by the enemy upon the wagon and ammunition train of his corps, Steele gathered up a force of stragglers and others, assumed command, and though himself a staff officer, attacked and dispersed the enemy's forces, thus saving the train. He received the medal on September 28, 1897. Following Colonel Steele's death, the medal was passed down from generation to generation. Until his death in 2016, it was in the possession of **John Ogden Whedon's** son, **Tom.** Thus, in all probability, it is now in the possession of one of his five sons.

Jon Stone, born in 1931, helped to create *Sesame Street* and developed the characters of Cookie Monster, Oscar and Big Bird. He wrote the show's pilot script, was the series original head writer and over the years won eighteen Emmy Awards as writer, producer and director.

Jon Stone was born in New Haven, Connecticut and after attending the Pomfret School, matriculated at Williams College in Williamstown, Massachusetts. Williams has an extensive theater program and upon graduation in 1952, he moved on to graduate studies at Yale University's School of Drama, earning a master's degree three years later. From there Stone went to New York City, where he entered a CBS training program and then embarked on a career in the world of children's television as a writer on that network's *Captain Kangaroo.* There, he met **Tom Whedon,** who years later he brought in as the original head writer of *The Electric Company.* In the intervening years, Stone had an opportunity to perform as well, in **Tom Whedon**'s off-Broadway musical cabaret, *Money.* Jon Stone died in 1997 at the age of sixty-five of ALS. In his *New York Times* obituary, Joan Ganz Cooney, well known as one of the other creators of *Sesame Street,* described him as, "probably the most brilliant writer of children's television in America."

Television: In 1946, only eight thousand United States homes had television sets. Yet four years later, with television beginning to replace radio as the dominant broadcast medium, twenty percent of American households had TVs. And a decade later, that figure reached ninety percent, representing 45.7 million American households.

Texas Li'l Darlin' centers on an editor, upset with the Republican's defeat in 1948 and his determination to find a candidate to rejuvenate the party's image. Thus, he sends his top emissary to Texas, where he discovers a patriotic figure whose campaign slogan is simply "Texas, Li'l Darlin'." The show touches on themes of politics, leadership, and democracy.

The Electric Company was an educational children's television series produced by the Children's Television Workshop. It aired on PBS over a period of six years, from October 25,1971 to April 15, 1977. **Tom Whedon** was brought on board by his good friend and colleague, *Sesame Street's* **Jon Stone**, during the show's developmental period and served as the series' first head writer. Created for the "graduates of *Sesame Street*", the series provided entertaining programming to help children develop their grammar and reading skills. Unlike its predecessor, *Sesame Street*, which licensed its Muppet characters for merchandising, *The Electric Company* never had a unique brand or character that could be marketed in the same way. In fact, the only notable items that they licensed were comic books and a Milton Bradley board game. Thus, the show was cancelled in 1977 at the height of its popularity.

Jeremy Abbott Walsh, aka Jerry Walsh: John Ogden Whedon's nephew, was all of ten years old when *Marjorie's Hotrod Boyfriend* aired live on *The Great Gildersleeve*. His mother was John Ogden Whedon's sister Margaret Tenney Whedon (Walsh) aka **Marge**. His father was **Richard** J. Walsh, Jr.

Richard J. Walsh Jr., was married to John Ogden Whedon's sister, Margaret Tenney Whedon (aka **Marge**) and was the father of Jeremy Abbott Walsh (aka **Jerry Walsh**). As with many in his wife's family, he was a Harvard graduate and had a literary bent. Fresh out of college he went to work as a journalist at the *Buffalo Times*, in Buffalo, New York, but the paper closed down in 1939. And so with his family (**Marge** and **Jerry**), he moved to Belrose on New York's Long Island and went to work for the John Day Company, a small book publishing house founded by his father in 1926, which was named after an Elizabethan printer. Their motto -- "Arise, for it is Day". After his father's retirement, he headed John Day until he, himself, retired in 1974 and sold the company to Thomas Y. Crowell. Their most prolific authors were Irving Adler, well known for his books on science and mathematics, and Nobel Laureate Pearl S. Buck, who had married his father in 1935.

Daniel Clark Whedon, born in 1916, was **John Ogden Whedon's** youngest sibling. As an adult, Dan taught the craft of woodworking at a high school on New York's Long Island and had two very talented children -- a daughter who traveled the world performing in the chorus of the New York City Opera and a son who's a musician, author and poet.

Joseph Hill Whedon, (aka Joss), was born in 1964, the youngest of **Thomas Avery Whedon's** sons by his first marriage and grandson of **John Ogden Whedon**. He grew up in New York City and after three years at a boarding school in England, matriculated with the class of 1987 at Wesleyan College in Middletown, Connecticut. It is while there that he adopted the name Joss. After college he went to work as a television writer, starting with the series, *Rosanne*. In 1992, he developed a motion picture script for *Buffy the Vampire Slayer,* over which he had no control of anykind. But five years later he had the opportunity to resurrect *Buffy* as a TV series, where he served as executive producer – and this time, had total artistic control. Joss' screen writing projects have included *Toy Story,* for which he was nominated for an Academy Award, as well as the Marvel blockbuster, *The Avengers.* He has also written comic books and is known to have created musical compositions. Collectively, his works eventually made him an icon, with a cult following.

Julia Carroll Whedon, aka Jill was **John Ogden Whedon's** daughter. Four years younger than her brother Tom, she too was a talented writer. A Sarah Lawrence graduate and Woodrow Wilson Fellow, she wrote short stories and articles that appeared in such publications as *Harpers, Redbook, Ladies Home Journal, The New York Times Book Review* and the *Washington Post* and authored books titled, *Girl of the Golden West , Two and Two Together, A Good Sport,* and *The Fine Art of Ice Skating: An*

Illustrated History and Portfolio of Stars. In 1961 she married, and later was divorced from, film critic Richard Schickel and had two daughters, Erika (author, essayist and journalist) and Jessica. Jill died in 2016.

Margaret Tenney Whedon (Walsh), aka Marge, born in 1911, was **John Ogden Whedon's** sister. In 1934, she married **Richard** J. Walsh, Jr. and two years later, gave birth to a son, Jeremy Abbott Walsh aka **Jerry Walsh,** who was ten years old when *Marjorie's Hotrod Boyfriend,* bearing his name, aired live on NBC's *The Great Gildersleeve.* **Marge**, like John, grew up on Croydon Road in Jamaica Estates. She also vacationed at the Whedon farm in Litchfield, Connecticut, where, at eighteen, she had a serious automobile accident. There, the car full of friends she was driving crashed -- and the end result was a broken leg, for which she endured a lengthy recovery period, delaying her matriculation as a Freshman at Vassar.

Roger Denison Whedon, born in 1907**,** was one of **John Ogden Whedon's** two brothers. He, like his brother John, two years his senior, matriculated at Harvard. A talented writer, Roger, too, served on the board of the *Harvard Lampoon.* Tragically, he committed suicide on New Year's Eve 1930/1931. The following day, there was an article in the *New York Times* with the headline, "Aviator, 23, A Suicide; Found Life A Joke".

Thomas Avery Whedon (1932-2016) was the oldest of **John Ogden Whedon's** two children. In his teens, he attended Phillips Exeter Academy and upon graduation, matriculated with Harvard's class of 1957. While there, like his father before him, Tom was active in Hasty Pudding and co-wrote the book for one of their musicals – 1953's *Ad Man Out.* He was also active in the Harvard Radcliffe Dramatic Club, where he met, Lee Jeffries, a Radcliffe coed, who he married in 1959. After graduating from Harvard, Tom served in the military, where he was a reporter for *Stars* *and Stripes,* a daily newspaper, which reported on matters concerning members of the United States Armed Forces and their communities, with an emphasis on those serving outside the United States. But the theatrical experiences of his Harvard days remained with him. Thus, he wrote two musicals which eventually ran off-Broadway, one titled *All Kinds of Giants* (1961) and the other, *Money: A Musical Play for Cabaret* (1963).

In 1960, Tom and Lee's son Samuel was born and his brother, Matthew Thomas arrived two years later. That same year, Tom began to write for television's *Captain Kangaroo,* where one of his colleagues there was **Jon Stone**, who the following year performed in Tom's cabaret musical, *Money.* When Tom and Stone went to the bank to cash their first series paychecks, which carried the words, *Captain Kangaroo Account,* the teller refused them thinking it was „funny money'. Tom and his writing partner, Stone, became close friends and left the series after three years. In the meantime, Tom and Lee's third son arrived. Named **Joseph Hill Whedon**, decades later, he would change his given name to **Joss**. In 1969, Tom and Stone collaborated on a TV production titled, *Hey, Cinderella,* which featured Jim Henson's Muppets. And though 1970 found Tom writing for *The Dick Cavett Show,* he went back to scripting for children's television, when Stone, by now one of the producers of *Sesame Street,* brought him on board as head writer in the development of the series to be titled, *The Electric Company.* It premiered in the Fall of 1971. Not long after, there were rifts in Tom and Lee's marriage, so they separated and eventually divorced.

In 1974, Tom married Pamela Merriam Webber, an *Electric Company* script supervisor and the following year they moved out of New York City to Pacific Palisades, California. Their move was followed by the birth of two sons – Jed in 1975 and Zachary four years later, who like their grandfather, father and brother Joss, also write for TV. Once out on the West Coast, writing opportunities for Tom abounded as both writer and producer.

There he became well known for sitcoms such as *Alice, Benson, It's a Living* and *The Golden Girls,* among others, garnering two Daytime Emmy Awards *(Between the Lions and The Electric Company)* and a Prime Time Emmy for *The Golden Girls.* Tom Whedon died March 23, 2016 at the age of 83.

Bibliography

Whedon-Wheadon-Wheaton Family Address List - compiled by Rev. H.C. Whedon, D. D. of Carthage, New York (date unknown)

Family Search.com: Church of the Latter Day Saints

IMDb - John Whedon's Television and Movie Credits

IMDb - Joss Whedon's credits as producer, writer and director

IMDb - Tom Whedon: Television Credits; Daytime Emmy Awards & Primetime Emmy Awards

MyHeritage.com

Scroll and Key Membership Directory, 1842-1979

The Great Gildersleeve. Volume 9 - Radio Archives

Vassar College, Office of the Registrar

Wikipedia

1/2/1931   "Flier, 23, A Suicide; Found Life a Joke" *New York Times*

1/29/1947   *The Great Gildersleeve*, GG470129 *Marjorie's Hotrod Boyfriend*

1947	*The Genealogy and History of the Denison and Whedon Families* by Burt Denison Whedon, Published privately for his grandchildren
1/27/1958	*Look Homeward Angel*'s (Playbill)
1963	*Money, A Musical Play for Cabaret*, book and lyrics by Tom Whedon and David Axelrod; Music by Sam Pottle © 1963 & © 1964 (Dramatist Play Service, Inc.)
7/17/1971	*It's Strictly Sandwiches at the Desk: A Day in the Life of Dick Cavett's Writers Really Isn't Much Fun.* (TV Guide)
1972	*The Big Broadcast (1920-1950)* a new, revised and greatly expanded edition of *Radio's Golden Age - The Complete Reference Work* by Frank Buxton and Bill Owen, Introduction by Henry Morgan. © 1966 and 1972, Pages 130-131 (Viking Press)
1972	*On Stage at the Palace for McGovern & Shriver,* Advertisement in the *New York Times,* listing Tom Whedon as one of the writers.
1973	*Girl of the Golden West* by Julia Whedon (Charterhouse)
11/27/1991	John Ogden Whedon's Obituary, *NY Times*

1998   *On The Air - The Encyclopedia of Old Time Radio* by John Dunning, Pages 293-296 (Oxford University Press)

2002   *The Great Gildersleeve* by Charles Stumpf and Ben Ohmart (BearManor Media)

2003   *Gildy's Scrapbook - Letters, Photos & Other Novelties on the Great Gildersleeve.* (BearManor Media, 2021); introduction by Page Peary

9/11/2004   Obituary of Susan Delray Whedon (Gannon Funeral Home)

2005   *Archives of the Airwaves, Volume 2,* Pages 223-224 (BearManor Media)

2014   *Joss Whedon - The Biography*, by Amy Pascale, Pages 9-18 (Chicago Review Press)

3/25/2016   Tom Whedon's obituary. *Hollywood Reporter*

2018   *Drunk in the Woods* by Tony Whedon, Page 114 (Green Writers Press)

2020   *The Two Great Gildersleeves* by Dan McGuire (BearManor Media)

2021   *The Big Hurt - A Memoir* by Erika Schickel (Hatchette Books)

About the Author

The Audiobook version of PEGGY ADLER's most recent title, *Trilogy: Three True Stories of Scoundrels and Schemers*, narrated by Peter Coyote, has won gold medals in two prestigious literary competitions. First in the Independent Publisher (IPPY) Book Awards competition and then in the Electronic Literature (eLit) Awards Competition. Prior to "*Trilogy*", she authored the historical biography, *Pallenberg Wonder Bears - From the Beginning* and the award winning pictorial history titled, *Images of America CLINTON*. Decades earlier, In the 1960s and 70s, Ms Adler authored and illustrated five titles for New York City publishers (The John Day Company & Franklin Watts), which went out of print in the mid-1980s -- and were republished in two volumes in 2023. Furthermore, she's illustrated two dozen others and provided art for the Bronx Zoo; the Humane Society of the United States; Little, Brown & Company; the Journal of Theoretical Biology; the Journal of Algebra; the National Council of Teachers of Mathematics; and World Scientific Publishing. Ms Adler also coordinated the 1969 world premiere of *Butch Cassidy and the Sundance Kid* for 20th Century Fox and worked as a consultant for the U.S. House of Representatives' *October Surprise Task Force*. Previous to winning the 2024 gold medals for *Trilogy*, her book *Images of America Clinton* was named "Best Research Publication" by the Connecticut Society of Genealogists. And in 2017, *Marquis Who's Who* presented her with their Albert Nelson Marquis Lifetime Achievement Award. Other honors include the Association of Former Intelligence Officer's General Richard G. Stilwell Award, the Duck Island Yacht Club's Corinthian Award and being named as a 2025 Connecticut Beacon Awardee. An active member of each community in which she's ever lived, she spent eight years as a Clinton, CT Police Commissioner and is presently Chairman of the town's Historic District Commission.